The Scale Of... TRAVEL

By Joanna Brundle

BookLife
PUBLISHING

©2019
BookLife Publishing Ltd.
King's Lynn
Norfolk PE30 4LS

All rights reserved.
Printed in Malaysia.

A catalogue record for this book is available from the British Library.

ISBN: 978-1-78637-881-1

Written by:
Joanna Brundle

Edited by:
Emilie Dufresne

Designed by:
Jasmine Pointer

All facts, statistics, web addresses and URLs in this book were verified as valid and accurate at time of writing. No responsibility for any changes to external websites or references can be accepted by either the author or publisher.

Photocredits

All images courtesy of Shutterstock.com. With thanks to Getty Images, Thinkstock Photo and iStockphoto.

Front Cover – Emilia Ennessy, Colorlife, Ekaterina Kiriy, VectorSMD, Tancha, Mr. Luck, Krylovochka. 2–3 – natashanast. 4–5 – MicroOne, Sunnydream, Tanakax3, darsi. 6–7 – bilha golan, intararit, ONYXprj, Shtonado, avh_vectors. 8–9 – A7880S. 10–11 – AnnstasAg, Macrovector, Vector Icon Flat, Guaxinim. 12–13 – Sira Anamwong, N.MacTavish. 14–15 – robuart. 16–17 – natashanast, Janos Levente, Dzianis_Rakhuba, Pompaem Gogh, Bobrik74. 18–19 – Derplan13, robuart. 20–21 – Ziablik, eveleen, Bur_malin. 22–23 – Amanita Silvicora, Lorelyn Medina, Sunnydream.

CONTENTS

Page 4	Introduction
Page 6	The Wright Brothers' Flights and the Marathon
Page 8	The Marathon and the Race to the South Pole
Page 10	The Race to the South Pole and the Tour de France
Page 12	The Tour de France and Route 66
Page 14	Route 66 and Crossing the Atlantic Ocean
Page 16	Crossing the Atlantic Ocean and the Trans-Siberian Railway
Page 18	The Trans-Siberian Railway and Amy Johnson's Flight
Page 20	Amy Johnson's Flight and Apollo 11's Flight to the Moon
Page 22	Apollo 11's Flight to the Moon and Mars Landing
Page 24	Glossary and Index

Words that look like <u>this</u> can be found in the glossary on page 24.

INTRODUCTION

The scale of things means how one thing compares in size to another. In this book, we will be travelling around the world and even into space, comparing the distances that people have travelled.

Some of the people that we shall be thinking about made their journeys by taking part in famous competitions. Others wanted to <u>explore</u> the world or to try out new ways of travelling. Let's start comparing.

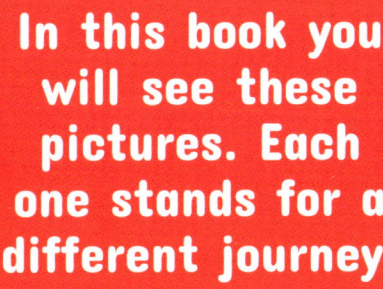

In this book you will see these pictures. Each one stands for a different journey.

 Wright Brothers' flights

 Marathon

 Amundsen's <u>expedition</u>

 Tour de France

 Route 66

 Atlantic Ocean

 Trans-Siberian Railway

 Amy Johnson's flight

 Apollo 11

THE WRIGHT BROTHERS' FLIGHTS AND THE MARATHON

> Wilbur and Orville helped their plane to fly by copying the shape of birds' wings.

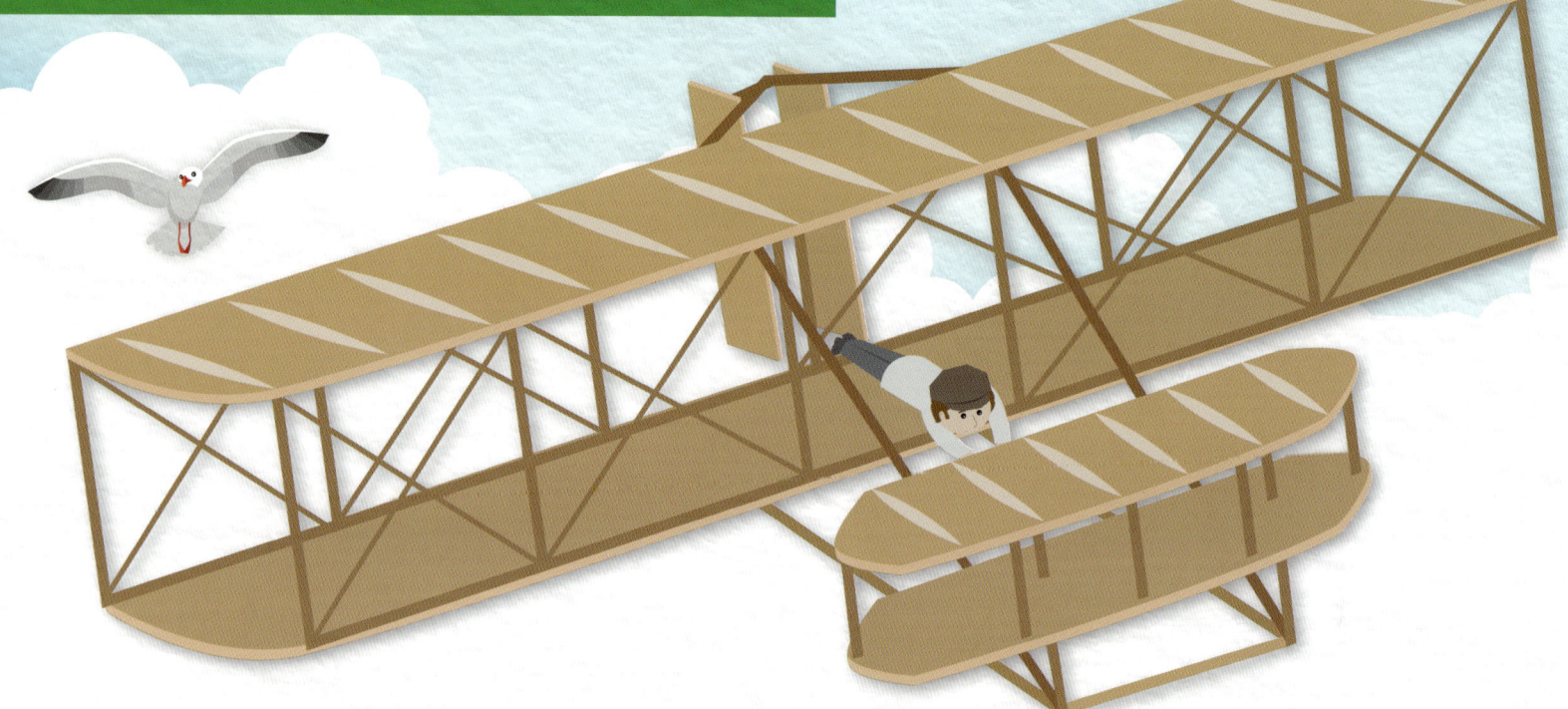

Wilbur and Orville Wright were American <u>inventors</u>. On the 17th of December, 1903, they made the first ever flights in a plane with an engine. On the fourth flight, Wilbur flew almost 260 metres.

260 metres

The marathon is a long-distance race. People taking part run, walk or use a wheelchair to travel just over 42 kilometres. That's over **160 TIMES** farther than Wilbur Wright's famous flight.

42 kilometres

THE MARATHON AND THE RACE TO THE SOUTH POLE

Many cities, including London, New York and Beijing, hold a marathon each year.

It is said that the first ever marathon was run in ancient Greece. A <u>messenger</u> ran from the city of Marathon to the city of Athens with news that a battle had been won.

46 kilometres ↔

2,600 kilometres ←

Roald Amundsen led the first expedition that reached the South Pole. The journey from the Bay of Whales in Antarctica to the South Pole and back again covered around 2,600 kilometres. That is the distance of almost 62 marathons.

South Pole

1,300 kilometres each way

Antarctica

Bay of Whales

THE RACE TO THE SOUTH POLE AND THE TOUR DE FRANCE

Roald Amundsen was a Norwegian explorer of both the North and South Poles. His expedition to the South Pole in 1911 turned into a race against an English explorer called Robert Scott. Amundsen won.

3,500 kilometres

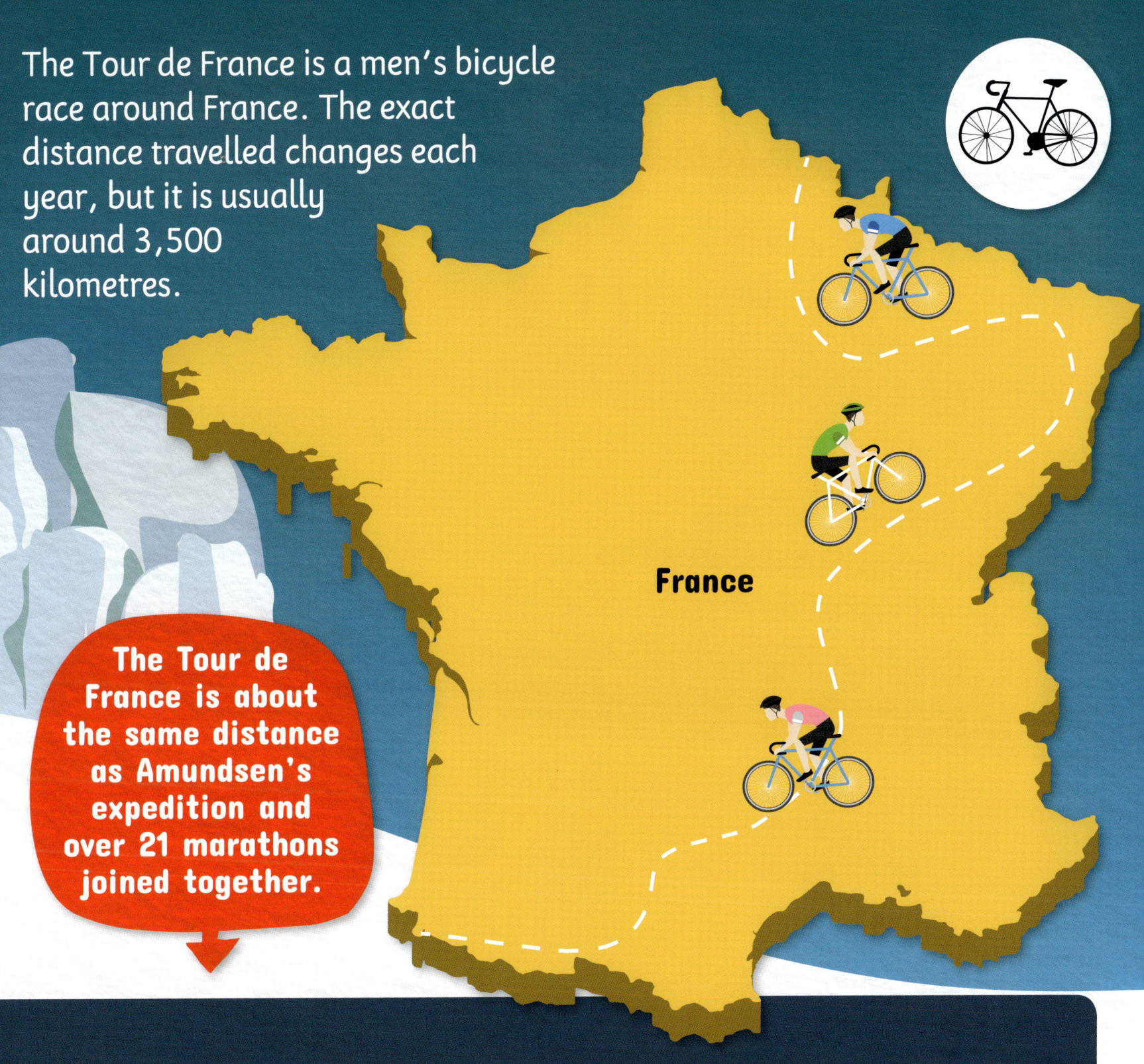

The Tour de France is a men's bicycle race around France. The exact distance travelled changes each year, but it is usually around 3,500 kilometres.

The Tour de France is about the same distance as Amundsen's expedition and over 21 marathons joined together.

THE TOUR DE FRANCE AND ROUTE 66

The number of people who watch the race around the world is the highest for any yearly sporting event.

The first Tour de France was held in 1903. The race usually happens over 23 days each July. The overall leader of the race at any of the 21 different stages wears a yellow jersey for the next stage.

Route 66 is a famous road in the US. It is around 3,665 kilometres long. That's about as far as a Tour de France and four marathons joined together.

3,665 kilometres

ROUTE 66
AND CROSSING THE ATLANTIC OCEAN

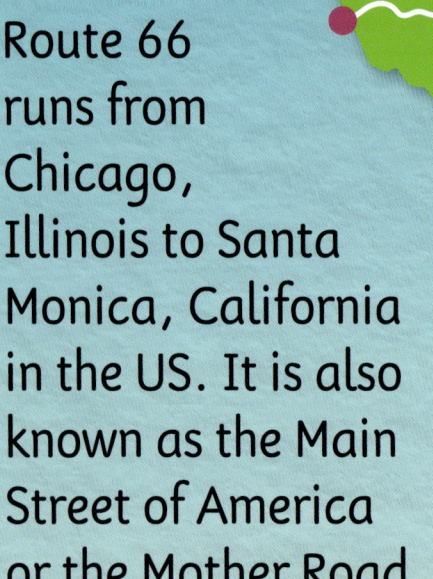

Route 66 runs from Chicago, Illinois to Santa Monica, California in the US. It is also known as the Main Street of America or the Mother Road.

The distance across the Atlantic Ocean from Southampton in England to New York in the US is over 5,500 kilometres. That is about **ONE AND A HALF TIMES** as long as Route 66 or the distance of 131 marathons.

Southampton

5,500 kilometres

5,800 kilometres

Paris

Atlantic Ocean

In 1927, Charles Lindbergh was the first person to fly <u>solo</u> across the Atlantic from New York to Paris, France.

3,665 kilometres

5,500 kilometres

Crossing the Atlantic Ocean and the Trans-Siberian Railway

People cross the Atlantic Ocean by plane and by ship. A man called Ben Lecomte is believed to have swum across the Atlantic Ocean in 1998. His journey covered 5,980 kilometres and took 73 days.

It took Lecomte **52 TIMES** as long to swim the distance as it did for Charles Lindbergh to fly.

5,500 kilometres

9,300 kilometres

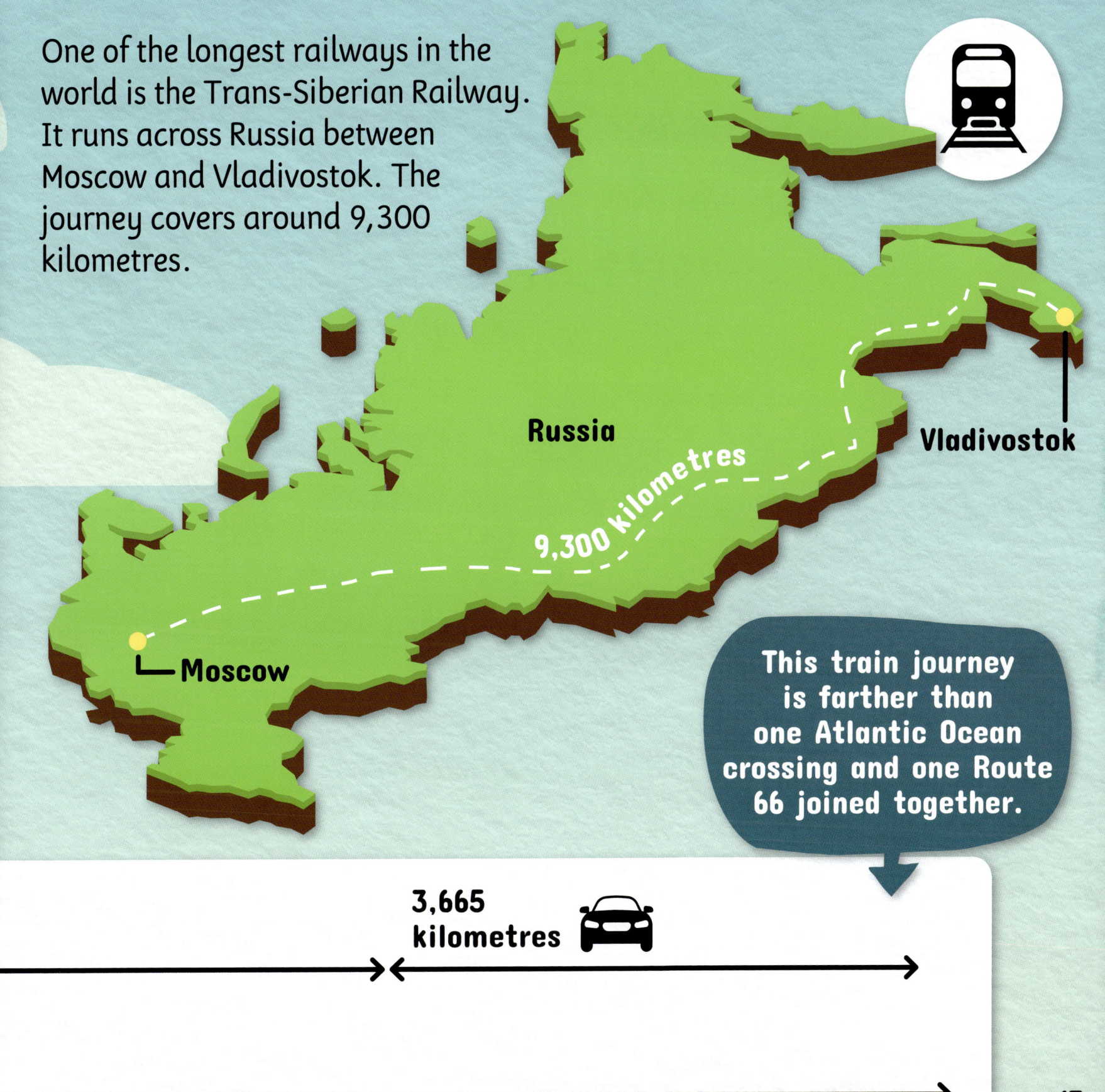

THE TRANS-SIBERIAN RAILWAY AND AMY JOHNSON'S FLIGHT

It takes over six days to complete the train journey from Moscow to Vladivostok. The train travels through mountains and forests and passes the biggest <u>freshwater</u> lake in the world.

9,300 kilometres

17,700 kilometres

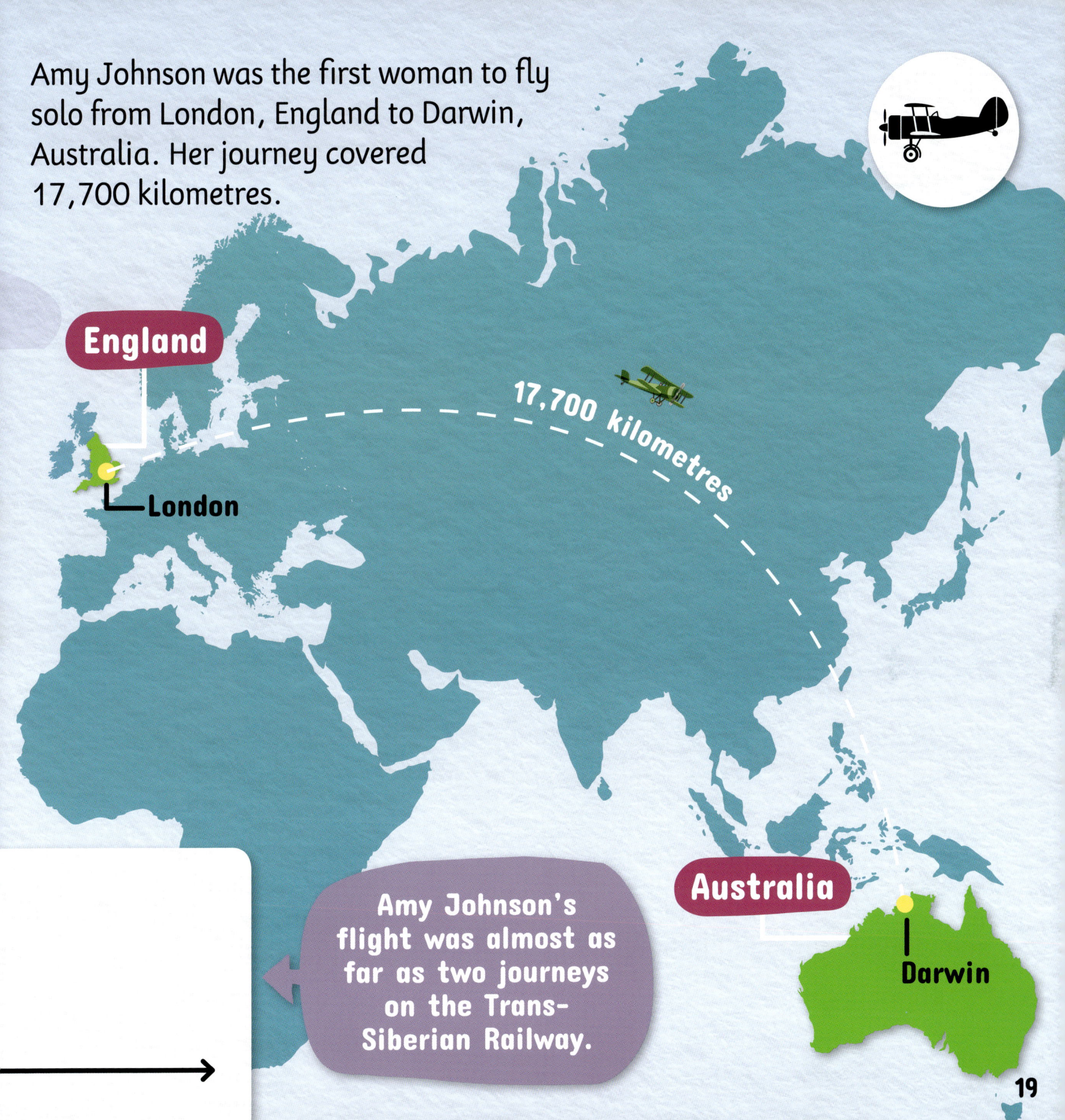

Amy Johnson's Flight and Apollo 11's Flight

Amy Johnson had no radio link to talk with anyone on the ground and only had basic maps to follow.

Amy Johnson took off from London on the 5th of May, 1930 and landed in Australia 19 days later. Her plane was second-hand and was called Jason.

17,700 kilometres
⟷

384,000 kilometres
⟵

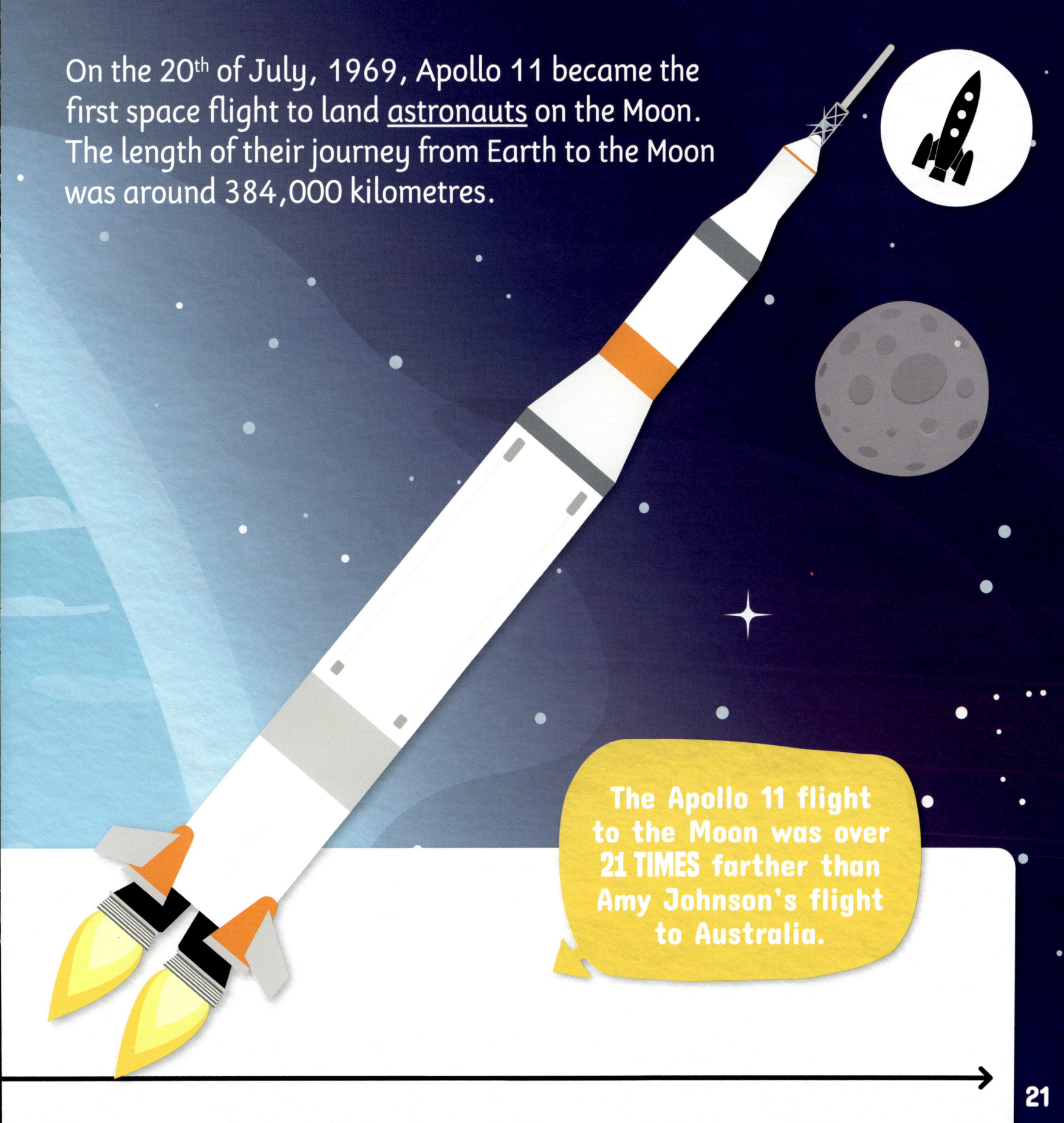

On the 20th of July, 1969, Apollo 11 became the first space flight to land <u>astronauts</u> on the Moon. The length of their journey from Earth to the Moon was around 384,000 kilometres.

The Apollo 11 flight to the Moon was over **21 TIMES** farther than Amy Johnson's flight to Australia.

Apollo 11's Flight
to the Moon and
Mars Landing

Neil Armstrong and Buzz Aldrin were the first men to walk on the Moon. Millions of people around the world watched on television. A plaque was left on the Moon, saying "We came in peace for all mankind."

The astronauts took rocks and dust from the Moon back to Earth for scientists to study.

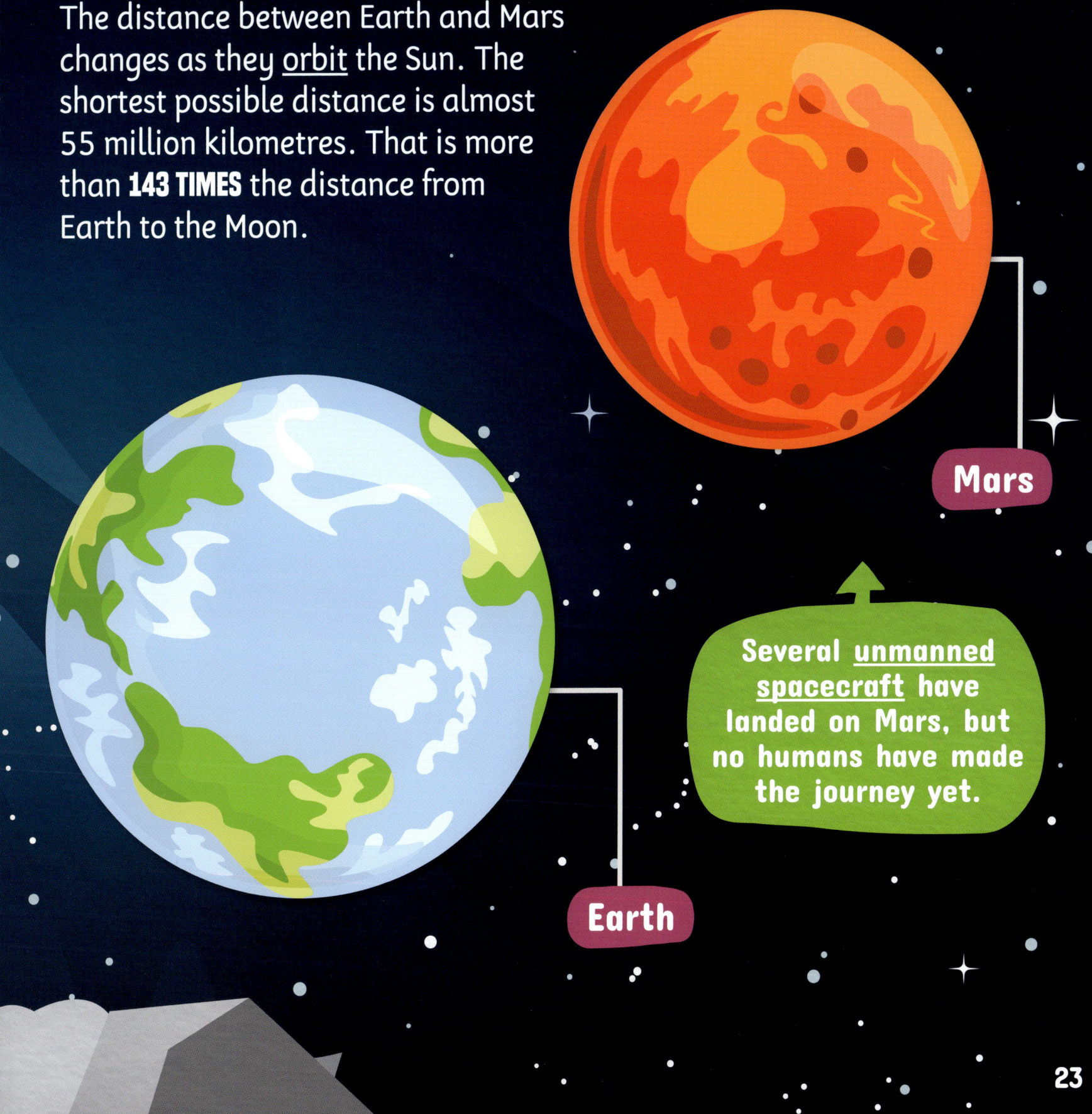

The distance between Earth and Mars changes as they <u>orbit</u> the Sun. The shortest possible distance is almost 55 million kilometres. That is more than **143 TIMES** the distance from Earth to the Moon.

Mars

Several <u>unmanned spacecraft</u> have landed on Mars, but no humans have made the journey yet.

Earth

GLOSSARY

astronauts	people who have been trained for space travel
expedition	a journey made by a group of people with a particular purpose, such as exploration
explore	travel to and find out about new or undiscovered places
freshwater	water that is not salty
inventors	people who create or design something that has never been seen before
mankind	the whole of the human race
messenger	someone who delivers news or instructions from one person or group to another
orbit	move in a curved path around a star or planet
plaque	a flat piece of a material such as wood or metal that is fixed to a wall or other surface, to remember a person or something that has happened
scientists	people who study and know a lot about the world
solo	done by one person on their own
unmanned spacecraft	vehicles used for travelling in space that are steered and controlled from the ground and do not have any humans on board

INDEX

Aldrin, Buzz 22
Amundsen, Roald 5, 9–11
Armstrong, Neil 22
astronauts 21–22
Earth 21–23
expeditions 5, 9–11

explorers 5, 10
Johnson, Amy 5, 19–21
Lecomte, Ben 16
Lindbergh, Charles 15–16
marathons 5, 7–9, 11, 13, 15
Mars 23

Moon 21–23
Scott, Robert 10
space 4, 21
Wright Brothers 5–7